The Net Interest Margin Solution

HOW TO ADD 40-50 BASIS POINTS IN THE NEXT 12 MONTHS

Roxanne Emmerich

Leadership Avenue Press
MINNEAPOLIS, MINNESOTA, USA

Copyright © 2014 Leadership Avenue Press.

All rights reserved. No part of this publication may be reproduced, distributed or transmitted in any form or by any means, including photocopying, recording, or other electronic or mechanical methods, without the prior written permission of the publisher, except in the case of brief quotations embodied in critical reviews and certain other noncommercial uses permitted by copyright law. For permission requests, write to the publisher, addressed "Attention: Permissions Coordinator," at the address below.

Leadership Avenue Press
8050 Washington Ave. S., Suite 100
Eden Prairie, MN 55344

Ordering Information:
Quantity sales. Special discounts are available on quantity purchases by corporations, associations, and others. For details, contact the "Special Sales Department" at the address above.

ISBN 978-1-890965-02-0

Additional FREE Tools and Resources Available at...

NetInterestMarginSolution.com/Resources

Go there right now to register and claim all your FREE gifts!

✓ Exclusive video reveals the "magic script" to break a prospect's preoccupation with rate so you can finally escape the 'what's your rate?' trap.

✓ Complete video case-study showing how one bank added 48 basis points to net interest margin. Discover what they did and how they did it.

✓ Specific, 'how-to' articles you can share with your key leaders in retail, marketing and commercial to jump-start your growth.

✓ PLUS: Priority notification of upcoming educational webinars to help you safely and rapidly grow profits and much more...

Contents

The Net Interest Margin Crisis 1

The Rate Matching Death Spiral 5

Why You Deserve to Get Treated Like a Commodity Peddler 9

The "Big Lie" About Low Rates 15

How to Attack The Root Cause of Net Interest Margin Compression 19

The Antidote to Commodity Hell 25

How to Get Premium Pricing on Every Product You Offer 33

5 Biggest Marketing Mistakes Made by Almost Every Bank That Kill Your Chances of GROWING Net Interest Margin 43

The Secret Marketing Approach That High-Performing Banks Don't Want You to Know 51

7 Deadly Sales Mistakes That Crush Your Margin 57

The 1-Step System Used by Top Banks To Snap *Rate Shoppers*" Out of Their Preoccupation With Low Rates . 65

How One Bank Grew Net Interest Margin by 100 Basis Points in Little Over a Year 73

i

Praise for The Emmerich Group

"You Will See My New $2,000,000 Loan Package Next Monday"

"I don't impress easily...Since starting this program, I have a lender that applied these powerful tools with a tough prospect he had been working on and, in short, sent me an email in bold that said, 'THIS STUFF REALLY WORKS!!!! By the way, you will see my new $2,000,000 loan package next Monday."

—Chuck Withee, President, The Provident Bank

"Are you working with The Emmerich Group yet? If you're not, you should."

—K. Burgess, Chairman, FirstCapital Bank of Texas
Former Chair of the ABA Community Bankers Council

"Revenue Grew From $12.2 Million to $25 Million"

"In the last six years of working with you, we've grown from $264 to $555 million—an annual compounded

growth rate of 11%, revenue grew from $12.2 million to $25 million, our employee engagement index is strong. Our Net Promoter Score is 9.04. The annual strategic plans have really helped us stay focused. The key initiatives and key indicators we developed to measure our progress are extremely valuable to our senior management team."
—P. Tieskoetter, President and CEO, Eastwood Bank

"Profits Are Up 44%!"

"I've attended Profit-Growth Banking™ Summit THREE times, sent ALL my managers, and in the last year since we've been implementing what we learned, we've experienced more growth than in the previous five years combined! The growth of deposits and loans can only be described as a miracle and profits are up 44%!"
—P. Steele, President and CEO, First Volunteer Bank

"Roxanne's System Works"

"I've always said that if our competitors got ahold of Roxanne's information, we'd be in trouble. Fortunately, we found her first.

Roxanne's system works— especially during times like these."

—A.Tubbs, CEO Ohnward Bancshares, Past President of American Bankers Association

"100 Percent of Our New Loan Customers Are Referrals"

"We grew 21 percent while decreasing FTEs by 11 percent and raising net interest margin 52 basis points since working with The Emmerich Group.

100 percent of our new loan customers are referrals from current customers or centers of influence.

Not a week goes by when I don't get a call from a client complimenting my staff. I don't even remember it happening before we made this shift.

Our top 100 customers are sending business our way, and we're not really having to work hard to get new business.

And our lenders don't even try or ask to meet the pricing of the competition. They know they're worth more. A few years ago, they wouldn't have believed they were worth the extra money."

—K. Miller, President and CEO, The Farmers Bank

"The Additional Cross-Sales We're Getting Are Amazing"

"The day after attending Profit- Growth Banking™, our CSR used the needs assessment techniques you taught with a customer opening a new account. Guess what? The customer pulled a $250,000 check from his billfold and opened an account! The additional cross-sales that are materializing are amazing. This is only a fraction of what's happening here since attending the event."

  —J. J. Blake, Regional President, MidSouth Bank

"Net income increased 87.26%"

"Net income increased 87.26%, earning assets grew 55.66%, and we have the lowest delinquencies in the state. Your help with focusing us on quality works."

  —G. Majors, CEO Hardin County Bank

"Boosted Net Interest Margin by Over 100 Basis Points in Our First Year!"

"We increased our ROA and boosted net interest margin by over 100 basis points each, in less than 18 months.

The culture change has transformed our bank. Our CFO, who heads our Hoopla Team®, now thinks the sky is the limit. Everybody who goes to the Profit-Growth Banking™ event comes back saying, „This changed the way I think in my personal life, too.'"

  —K. Beckemeyer, President and CEO, Legence Bank

About Roxanne Emmerich

Roxanne Emmerich is the CEO of The Emmerich Group®, a Minneapolis-based company that helps community banks create performance transformations to take them to a level of performance they never even dreamed possible. Roxanne has helped many banks get to and stay in the top 5% of performance. She is the author of 5 books including the *New York Times* and *Wall Street Journal* bestseller, *Thank God It's Monday!*® and the top-selling book in banking, *Profit-Growth Banking*™. For more information on how to become, and remain, a top-performing bank, visit www.EmmerichFinancial.com.

To have Roxanne or one of our other team members speak to your group or to inquire about working directly with The Emmerich Group to transform your bank's results call (952) 820-0360 or send an email to Pat@EmmerichGroup.com.

INTRODUCTION

The Net Interest Margin Crisis

There's a great suffering...a gnashing of teeth...happening in banking right now, as you read this.

Right now in an office somewhere on mainstreet in your town there's a bank CEO holed up in a conference room with a few of his executives. Yes, this very minute, they're looking at each other across the table, lined with bagels and coffee...waiting.

Waiting and hoping that someone in that room has an answer to the biggest problem they've faced since the Great Recession.

The bank is being crushed by price competition from banks up and down Main Street that are perfectly happy to lowball a rate. After all, you've got to get in the game and be competitive if you want to win the business.

This is the new way to run a bank.

So the meeting in the ~~bunker~~ boardroom goes on...

No one knows how to solve the crushing net interest margin compression that's...

- ✓ Chewing up your prospects for growing profits this year.
- ✓ Likely to create a bigger problem with earnings next year.
- ✓ Eating away at the capital you desperately need to weather the storms and grow to meet your board's expectations.
- ✓ Causing the board to look at you without holding eye contact as they contemplate replacing you.
- ✓ Causing your most vocal board member to have meetings outside your meetings where he repeats his new refrain "Enough Already".

EmmerichFinancial.com

CHAPTER 1

The Rate Matching Death Spiral

"Round and 'round we go, where we stop nobody knows."

In most banks today the CLO's office needs to be fitted with a revolving door to accommodate all the lenders streaming in pleading to match rates with a low-ball competitor.

They come in saying, "We have to get competitive to win the business."

And they're persuasive, compelling and too often...successful in convincing the CLO to bend just *one more time*.

Funny they aren't more convincing in front of the customer (more on that in a moment).

Now, when you look at it up close, one deal at a time, matching a rate to acquire a good customer "could" be a good idea. But it's not happening on just one deal in most banks.

It's happening on the majority of deals.

And when you backup and look at the big picture you see that you're trapped in the Rate Matching Death Spiral.

Here's how it works...

Customer goes to First Bank, where they have an account. First Bank offers them a rate of 6.5%. Customer thinks, "That's a good rate, but I better do my due diligence to make sure."

So they go to Second Bank. Second Bank offers them a rate of 6.00%. Customer thinks, "That's good, but I have an account at First Bank. I wonder if they'll beat that price." So they go back to First Bank and ask.

Back at First Bank, the lender now knows he's in a competitive situation. He pleads his case to "get competitive." After all he argues, "If we lose this loan, we might lose the other accounts the customer has with us. We need to match the rate, or better, to keep this customer!"

So he goes back to the customer and offers a rate of 6.00%.

And the customer says, "Great! Let's go."

Feeling like the victor, the lender announces that he's won the business!

And the CEO silently groans..."At what cost?"

Back at Second Bank, they're licking their wounds. They had the better rate and still lost. "We'd better

sharpen our pencils and get even more competitive next time!"

And the next time out they go below 6%. And First Bank matches.

The Rate Matching Death Spiral continues down, down, down. And nobody knows where it stops...it only stops when you wake up and confront the reasons why you feel compelled to match your competitors' rates.

CHAPTER 2

Why You Deserve to Get Treated Like a Commodity Peddler

Ok...this may sound harsh, but if I'm not brutally honest with you, who will be?

If you're feeling the pressure to match rates, you're a commodity peddler.

And if your lenders can't get deals at premium prices, you and they deserve what comes with matching those rates.

The market always pays the peddler what the peddler deserves. If your prospects can get the exact same loan or account across the street for a better rate, they will, and they should.

It's your job to give them a reason, other than price, to do business with you. Throughout the rest of this book I'm going to show you a system to do just that. But first, we need to deal with the heart of the problem.

Being in the commodity business is a choice.

That's good news and...*bad news.*

The bad news is that, if you're there, it's the simple and predictable result of the choices you've made until now. It means that you have not created any real, tangible reason for customers to do business with you that *they* actually care about.

And here's the rub...

You may think you've given them reasons. But if one of them is "we've been in the community for 113 years" and the other is "we're focused on great customer service" you're fooling yourself.

Maybe some nice little old lady cares because her father was a customer a century ago and she has fond memories, but that's it.

Outside of the top 5% banks (and those that are zooming to that level), the rest of industry has no idea why customers choose one bank over another. Don't beat yourself up...it's an industry-wide epidemic. And according to a recent piece in *Fast Company* magazine it's about to get even worse as the Millennials start putting their money outside of banks altogether.

Fast Company published the results of a study of Millennials by Viacom Media. Here's what Millennials had to say about banks:

- ✓ 53% don't think their bank offers anything different than other banks.
- ✓ 71% would rather go to the dentist than listen to what banks are saying.
- ✓ All 4 of the leading banks are among the 10 least loved brands by Millennials. (Yes, our industry holds 4 of the top 10 LEAST popular brands!)
- ✓ 68% say that in 5 years, the way we access our money will be totally different. (Meaning, they're looking for something to replace you.)
- ✓ 70% say that in 5 years, the way we pay for things will be totally different. (Who needs a checking account?)
- ✓ 33% believe they won't need a bank at all. (Are you prepared to see 1/3 of the next generation opt-out of the banking system?)
- ✓ Nearly half are counting on tech start-ups to overhaul the way banks work. (They've grown up with PayPal…and believe that tech is better equipped to deliver the value they want.)
- ✓ 73% would be more excited about a new offering in financial services from GOOGLE, AMAZON, APPLE, PAYPAL or SQUARE than from their own bank.

Of the six industries studied the risk of disruption for banking was almost double that of all the others.

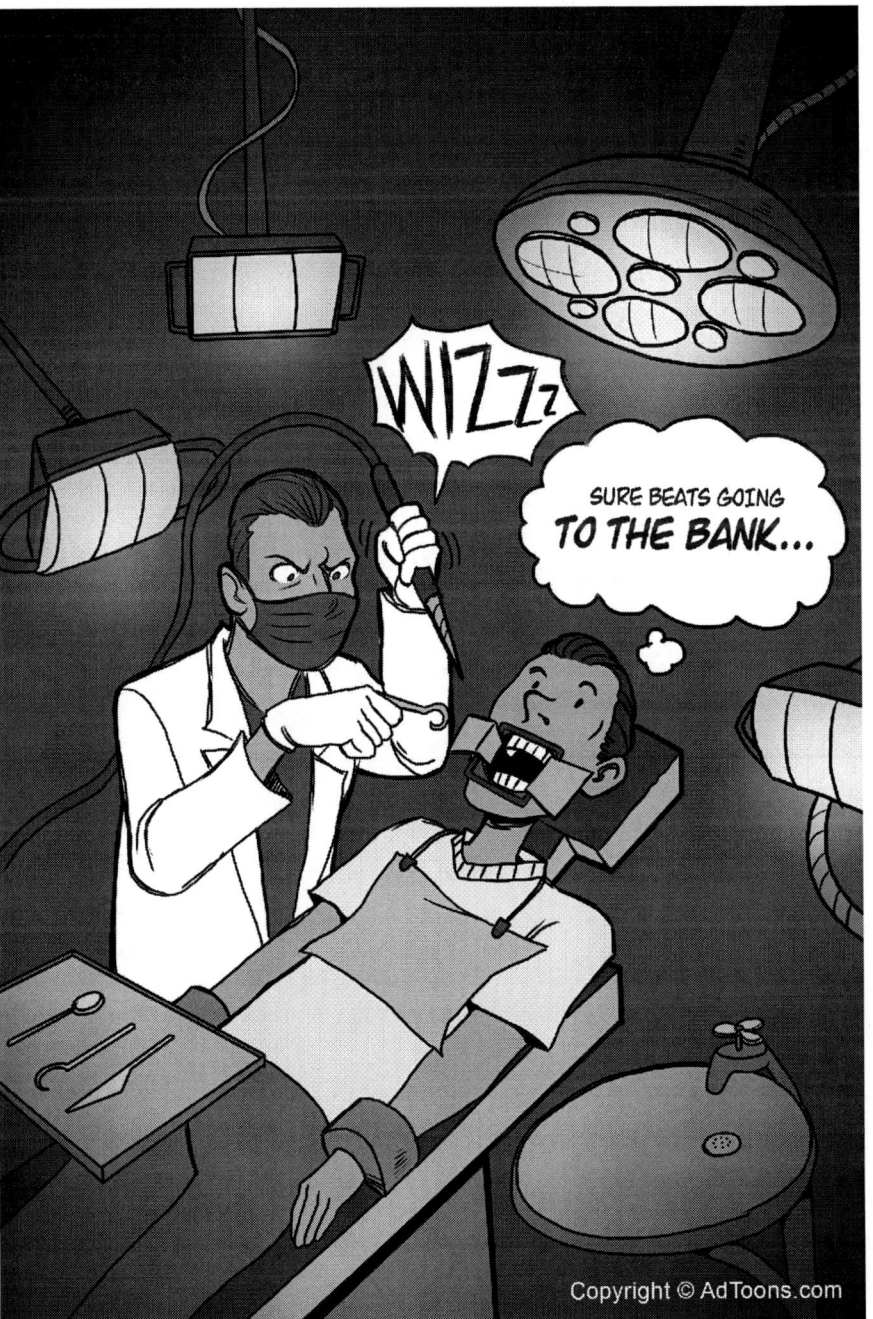

If you have to match rates to win business from Baby Boomers (age 50+) and Gen X (ages 30-50)...and both groups still believe in banking. JUST WAIT...the Millennials are moving into the market and a big number of them see no need for bankers.

Shame on us for not giving them some good reasons to value what we do as an industry.

The good news is...you *can* make a different choice.

And the change doesn't take long. I've worked with hundreds of banks. Most were good banks, but not necessarily top-performers when we started working together. And within a year or two of applying the system I'll reveal, they added 50, 100 even 150 basis points to their margin. That kind of change transforms a bank and takes huge pressure off the CEO and executives. Oh, and it sure makes the Board happy too.

CHAPTER 3

The "Big Lie" About Low Rates

Let's get one thing straight. Low price IS a strategy. And consciously or unconsciously, every time you match rates to win business you're saying, "Our strategy is to be the lowest price bank in our market."

If you're going to go the low-price route, at least make a conscious decision to pursue that strategy rather than have it be the result of dozens or hundreds of little unconscious decisions to match rate. And, do it with the understanding of history...

Consider the history of the low price strategy in business.

Let's start with Sears. You may not know this, but Sears was the Wal-Mart of the late 1800s and early 1900s. They pioneered a breakthrough direct to consumer mail-order distribution model. The Sears Catalog had everything you ever wanted or needed: housewares, clothing, agricultural supplies, tools...even the house itself. And because of Sears' scale and distribution advantage they were able to negotiate price advantages and carry a greater variety than local stores (remind you of any modern companies?).

Then there was Montgomery-Ward...and F.W. Woolworth Company...more recently Kmart and of course...

Wal-mart.

Each of these companies expanded rapidly using a low-price strategy coupled with some other advantage that allowed them to sell at razor-thin margins. The problem with the low-price strategy is simple...someone's always crazy enough to undercut you. No matter how low you go.

And whatever operational advantage you create to allow you to grow on low margins, will, sooner-or-later be knocked off by the competition.

Then you're toast.

And just in case you're reading this thinking who could ever beat Wal-Mart, look quickly to Amazon. They can, they intend to, and they have the capacity to take down Wal-Mart.

Even Bezos, Amazon's CEO, says he's afraid for the longevity of Amazon...because he's a student of history.

So what's the point?

Simple...**if these icons of American business can't survive for the long-term on a low-price strategy, how is it that you expect to do it?**

Low price is death. Plain and simple. It's only a matter of time.

The #1 thing I want you to get from reading this little book is that the easiest way...the most reliable way...and the only proven way to survive and thrive in every economic environment is to follow a strategy of premium pricing.

In the rest of this book, I'll share the things you need to do to get premium pricing, but you must decide to follow the path.

CHAPTER 4

How to Attack The Root Cause of Net Interest Margin Compression

The constant "need" to match rates to win a deal is a symptom, not the cause of the net interest margin crisis in banking today. The cause is much deeper.

It's inside each of your lenders...and it may be inside of you. Frankly, it's not your fault (or theirs). It's unconscious and has been a limiting belief in the banking industry for at least 100 years (probably longer).

And don't worry, if you're frustrated with your margin, but feel you have to fight any way you can to keep the customers you have and get new ones, you're not alone. In fact, you're in the majority.

What you'll see in this short book is not the "majority approach," though it should be.

> *"Look at what the majority of people are doing, and do the exact opposite, and you'll probably never go wrong for as long as you live".* --Earl Nightengale

I'd like for you to reflect on that quote for a moment. Look around you. The *majority* of people are not wealthy. The *majority* of people are sub-par in terms of health. The *majority* of companies fail in the first 5 years. And, the *majority* of bankers are screaming about compressed margins.

Do what the majority does and get what the majority gets.

Are you doing what the majority of banks are doing right now?

Or, are you doing the things that the most successful banks are doing? The Top 5% banks?

I've invested the last 25-years of my life working with Top 5% banks, and taking banks that were no where near the Top 5% and getting them there within just a few years.

The top 5% performing banks operate very differently than the bottom 95%. And the difference starts with what I'm about to share with you.

Frankly, I'm concerned that if I do share it, you won't believe it. It may seem too simple. It may seem like something that's difficult to change (although it's not). You may think, sure, I can do it, but how will I ever get my lenders and the rest of my team to do it...I'll show you how.

The Real Reason You Match Rates

The root of the problem causing an industry-wide crushing of net margins isn't competition.

It isn't the economy.

It isn't the Fed.

It isn't even the meetings in Basel.

No, the root of the problem is in the limiting beliefs in minds of bankers, in banks across the country.

You see, if you don't believe you're worth a premium rate, you won't get a premium rate. If you don't believe you're worth a premium rate, your customer won't believe it either.

It all starts with fixing the beliefs about you, your bank, what you're selling and why it's valuable to people.

When Karen Miller, CEO of The Farmers Bank, was asked how she managed to grow net interest margin by 50 basis points, here's what she said: *"I think most significant was that we convinced our lenders that they, and The Farmers Bank, are worth the extra money."*

Yes, there are some new skills that you'll need to get out of the net interest margin crunch, but none of those skills will help if you and your people don't first change your limiting beliefs...and begin believing that you're worth premium prices.

You're probably thinking right now, "No, I want premium prices, but my loan is essentially the same as the next bank's. Why would anyone pay more for the same thing?"

You're right. They shouldn't pay more.

The trick is this...don't offer them the same thing as the next bank. Offer them more value. I'll show you how to do just that shortly.

EmmerichFinancial.com

CHAPTER 5

The Antidote to Commodity Hell

If you're feeling trapped in rate competition, you're in...Commodity Hell.

And it's not a fun place. When you're viewed by your customers and prospects as no different than the bank down the street, you create a situation where retaining customers and attracting new ones is beyond difficult.

The first reaction is to blame the customers. You've heard it at banking conventions before. Someone will complain about the sorry state of the consumer..."*Customers just don't care about relationship anymore. It's all about rates and fees.*"

That's backward thinking.

Yes, it is all about rates and fees *if* you don't give the customer any other good reason to use in making their decision. Notice the change...it's up to you to give them a good reason to choose you.

I know you're thinking, "But we do give them reasons to do business with us. When you come to our bank we have a friendly, service-focused staff." That's great, but it's not any different than what every other bank is saying. If you want different pricing—premium pricing—you've got to be delivering premium value. The same-old-same-old won't work.

The Secret to Unlocking Premium Pricing

If you want premium pricing you must be more valuable to a prospect (even at a higher rate) than another bank. And you've got to have a way to communicate your value to that prospect. You need a Unique Selling Proposition (USP).

Rosser Reeves, creator of the USP concept, in his book *Reality in Advertising* laments that the USP is widely misunderstood and defines it in three parts:

1. Each advertisement must make a proposition to the consumer—not just words, product puffery, or show-window advertising. Each advertisement must say to each reader: "Buy this product, for this specific benefit."

2. The proposition must be one the competition cannot or does not offer. It must be unique—either in the brand or in a claim the rest of that particular advertising area does not make.

3. The proposition must be strong enough to move the masses, i.e., attract new customers as well as potential customers.

Let's break that down and apply it to your bank.

#1. Reaves says, "each advertisement must say to each reader: 'Buy this product, for this specific benefit.'" Where Reeves says *advertisement*, think broadly. It means every place you promote a product or service to a customer or prospect—website, email, social media, signs and more traditional ads on TV, radio, print and direct mail. Every time you promote a product you MUST say to the consumer "Buy this product, for this specific benefit."

#2. The proposition must be one that your competition cannot or does not offer. In other words, it has to be unique. If not, there's no advantage in using it.

#3. The proposition must be strong enough to move the masses. It's not enough to talk about benefits, even unique benefits, if the benefits are weak and unimportant to your prospects.

Examples of Winning USPs

To help you get a sense of what a good USP sounds like, let's examine some you'll recognize.

Bank of America. During the 2002 Olympics Bank of America did a fantastic job of claiming a specific, unique and beneficial USP:

EmmerichFinancial.com

"There are some things we don't do very well, but we *have* figured out how to eliminate 80-percent of the up-front paperwork involved in mortgages."

That statement was played as a skier tumbled head over heels, down the slope on screen. Notice a couple of things about this USP. It's specific—they won't just save you some time, they've figured out how to cut 80% of the up-front paperwork in a mortgage application. Wow!

If you've ever sold a house and moved you know that it's a busy time. This is a direct and specific benefit, perfectly tuned to that customer. Now, to be fair, other banks may have reduced paperwork in a similar way. But, following Rosser Reeves definition of USP as long as it's a proposition that the competition does not offer (in other words, they don't promote the benefit), then it's unique.

And because Bank of America claimed it, they owned that position in the minds of the market.

Look at your marketing messages. Are you saying tangible things that matter to people?

Domino's Pizza. One of the single best examples of a USP that's ever existed is the one that launched Domino's to a leading position in the pizza business. For a number of reasons, they've abandoned this USP (a combination of liability related to fast driving delivery people and the competition knocking off the 'fast delivery' advantage) but it still stands as an excellent model:

Copyright © AdToons.com
UNIQUE SELLING PROPOSITION
USP
WE CAN DO IT!
GRAB IT!
COMMODITY HELL

"Fresh, hot pizza delivered to your door in 30 minutes or less--or it's free."

Notice, Domino's didn't promise your pizza would taste good. It didn't promise that it was made with the finest ingredients from an old world recipe passed down by Grandmama Domino. It only promised what was most important to the company's ideal customers—fresh, hot pizza in a hurry.

It worked because Dominoes asked a critical question:

'What do customers really want that our competitors aren't giving them?'

At that time, getting a pizza delivered meant waiting an hour or more and, when it arrived, it was as cold as the cardboard it came in.

FedEx. You think you have a tough competitive environment...When Fred Smith founded FedEx in 1971 he had one major competitor—The United States Postal Service, a government monopoly in the package delivery service.

Yet, FedEx's familiar USP turned the mail industry upside down:

"When it absolutely, positively has to be there overnight."

FedEx hit right at the heart of its competitor's weakness—slow, unreliable delivery. For the FedEx customer—business people shipping important packages and documents—this was music to their ears. Now, let me connect the dots for you...it currently costs 49-cents to send a First Class letter. Using the Postal Service's Priority Overnight mail you'll pay $19.99.

To ship FedEx Priority Overnight, the current rate is $58.20.

The FedEx USP is worth 118 times more than the First Class service and almost 3 times more than similar overnight delivery from the Postal Service.

Strong USPs unlock premium pricing.

EmmerichFinancial.com

CHAPTER 6

How to Get Premium Pricing on Every Product You Offer

It's not enough to have one USP for the bank. You have too many products and too many types of customers. You need one for the bank. And you need USPs for every one of your products, for each target group of customers.

Each USP is a golden thread that connects a tangible benefit that matters to that specific customer, to your product that delivers the benefit.

> Developing dozens of USPs may sound difficult. It doesn't have to be. In fact, I take bankers through the process at each of our Profit-Growth Banking™ Summits. If you want a shortcut, get to our next event pronto! Dates and locations are available at NetInterestMarginSolution.com/Summit.

When I'm working 1-on-1 with a client, I start with the question:

"When people come to you from another financial institution, what is the number one reason they switch?"

I'm not looking for why you think they switch. I want to know the exact words they use. If you don't know, ask. The words they use will reveal the position you hold in their minds (what they perceive that you offer that's different and more perfectly suited to them).

They'll also reveal your advantages over the competition. You want to find the places where your strengths match up against a competitor's weakness.

That's where you have competitive advantage and can claim a USP.

Here are some examples we've helped develop for our clients:

For Mortgage Departments:

Advantage over competition: Bank accepts and processes mortgages locally from application through closing vs. Competitor who accepts application locally and ships off the processing, leaving no one accountable to the customer.

USP: *"We hold your hand from application to closing. You'll never have to hassle with calling an 800 number in a far-away city where nobody cares. Nor will you have to deal with a closing where things go wrong and nobody is accountable."*

Advantage over competition: Bank services its own loans.

USP: *"Your loan will never be sold to a big-city bank that doesn't know you or doesn't answer the phone. And, if you have a problem with tax escrow, you won't destroy your credit rating as you spend months trying to talk to someone far away, who speaks a language you can't understand."*

For Trust Departments:

Advantage over the competition: In-house money managers.

USP: *"We have local money managers who can build a unique portfolio for you and your specific tax, growth and cash flow needs."*

Advantage over competition: Trust department does house calls.

EmmerichFinancial.com

USP: "*We come to your home or your business to save you time AND to understand all we can about your lifestyle and how we can make it better.*"

Each of these works because they are focused on something that matters to the customer. But that alone isn't enough. In each case, the benefit that matters is made tangible by giving specifics.

Here are a couple more...

One banker I know has a voicemail message that says: "*If I don't call you back within 27 hours, it's breakfast, lunch or dinner on me!*" That's a specific benefit, plus a guarantee (and I'll bet it's 100% unique).

Another bank has this guarantee: "*Through our drive-through in five minutes or we'll give you $50.*" Yep...it's a benefit that matters to customers, it's specific—5 minutes—and there's a guarantee, which makes it believable.

Oh, and here's the great thing about USPs...they force you to deliver! You'd better believe that getting customers through the drive-through in 5-minutes is a customer service focus at that bank. And I'll bet they've never paid that $50. So, they attract more customers and motivate staff to take great care of customers.

Not many banks are brave enough to do this, but these guys are laughing all the way to their own vault!

Copyright © AdToons.com
ROLEX
NO THANKS, I WANT THE REAL THING!
DISCOUNT ROLEX

If you don't have USP's you're not unique (by definition). So why would anyone pay a premium to do business with you?

You have two choices now: Continue on as you've been doing business, with weak, me-too, marketing messages and the price competition that comes with them. OR, you can start developing your USPs and give customers a reason to WANT to pay you more.

How to Leverage Your USPs for Higher Rates and Fees

Now that you've got them, it's time to put them to work for you.

Your USPs should be front and center in every form of communication with clients from your advertising, to your community outreach, to your internal and external signage and in every 1-on-1 conversation between your staff and your customers.

The fastest and easiest way to get your USPs in front of customers and prospects is to use them in your sales process. Start by drafting questions for each employee, based on their role or department.

Let's use the previous USP examples to build a few relevant questions.

The mortgage department that handles the entire mortgage process locally might ask:

"How important is it to have someone working with you from application to closing who insures that your mortgage processes easily and quickly, as opposed to most financial institutions, where, after they take your application, it goes into a far-off land to be processed and you're on your own if you have a problem?"

Now, read that again...

What prospect in their right mind would say *"No, it's not important at all?"* You'll get some no's...consider that good. Those are just prospects who aren't really serious or who ONLY value rate disqualifying themselves.

The overwhelming majority will say, *"Yes, of course, that's very important."* You've just driven a wedge between that customer and every other bank. Once they've agreed out loud that the benefit you offer is important, it's very difficult for them to contradict themselves and go somewhere else, unless they can find the very same benefit.

Oh, but they can't, because you created a UNIQUE Selling Proposition!

Another example...

For the bank that services its own mortgages:

"How important is it to you to have someone with whom you can talk locally if you have questions or concerns now or

in the future about your mortgage? Whereas most mortgages that are sold in the secondary market, you are given an 800-number—thus making it nearly impossible to find a human to answer a question for you."

For each product you might have two or three or four USPs. Each tied to a specific benefit. Here's why...individual customers are different. Some may find that one or two aren't important to them at all, but maybe the third one you share hits them right between the eyes...they have to have that benefit.

Arm yourself with all of your advantages.

For the trust department with in-house money managers:

"How important is it for you to work with a trust department that has individuals on-site, who make the investment decisions, so they can customize buys and sells to your tax situation?"

Notice, these are open-ended questions. Don't ask "Is it important to you..." that question requires a yes or no answer. You want to know *how important* that benefit is to the prospect. Asking in this way will get them to open up and tell you how to sell to them.

For the trust department that does house calls:

"How important is it for you to work with a trust company where the people who manage your most important assets get to know you personally and help YOU save time?"

Next roll out your USPs into your marketing, your referral systems, your advertising and your public relations efforts. They should be everywhere.

The Fastest Route to Getting Your USPs Done

Our 2-day Profit-Growth Banking™ Summit is the ultimate shortcut to creating your USPs.

This 2-day event walks you step by step through the USP process.

You'll actually create your USPs at the event and you'll hear USPs from top bankers in other markets for inspiration.

You even have access to our team of expert coaches to review and help you optimize your USPs.

Every Summit we've ever held has sold out. I recommend you immediately go to NetInterestMarginSolution.com/Summit for upcoming dates and availability.

EmmerichFinancial.com

CHAPTER 7

5 Biggest Marketing <u>Mistakes</u> Made by Almost Every Bank That Kill Your Chances of GROWING Net Interest Margin

Does this sound like your world?

Your marketing department is filled with "creatives"—they make things pretty, produce lots of "stuff," and throw great parties.

But, when it comes to proving out ROI, well...who wants to talk about that uncreative stuff, right?

Problem is, they're doing what they learned to do in marketing schools. But did you ever meet a marketing professor who made money with their marketing strategies? Are you wondering why Gallup found that "marketing executive" was the job title that was most often cut last year? Might there be a universal "ROI" challenge?

Your bank doesn't need more unprofitable customers. Why count the number of new accounts? It's not a numbers game. It's a profit game.

Exactly.

They teach branding, creativity, how to build slogans, how to order paraphernalia with logos on "stuff," how to do campaigns and product launches. All fine things.

And they worked just ducky a few years back, but these things haven't seen an ROI for well over a decade. Unfortunately, nobody's updated the teaching, so most banks get a negative ROI from what are often fairly large budgets.

It is a double tragedy—the money is wasted. But the real cost is *not getting* the most profitable customers at premium pricing. **That costs millions.**

What's the answer: Fire the people in marketing? Not at all. They just need some re-schooling about what is working now. It's not their fault. But, let's get this rolling in the right direction right now. No reason to wait.

So, what are the biggest wastes of marketing dollars today?

Mistake # 1. Branding
The "snake oil" of marketing

There is an inherent problem here. Everybody is spending ridiculous amounts of money on branding...but nobody knows what branding is.

Branding is not about having pretty logos, lobbies and brochures.

Think about it. When was the last time a $5 million customer with great credit walked in the door and said, "I'd sure like to pay you 100 to 200 basis points more because I *love* your logo"?

They don't come to you for the pretty things. They come because of your reputation for having an impeccable culture of people who are going to knock themselves out to make and save them money in creative ways that make sense. THAT is your brand. All the rest is snake oil.

Incidentally, just go to elance.com or CrowdSpring.com and put in bids for your logos, brochures and other pieces for $500 or less, and you'll get what you're paying $200,000 for. You can spend the rest on the real work of branding.

Mistake #2. Product Pushes

Bada bing bada boom! And let me show you the Special of the Day! Is that what a customer wants to hear from their bank--the people they come to as a source of wisdom to help them retire with financial independence?

Not a chance. But that's exactly how a product push comes off. So get over it. Marketing needs to understand that their role is to drive profit-rich "non salesy" selling in their organization in such a way that they get entire relationships at premium pricing.

Anything less than that will lower your perception to that of a salesy pusher of financial "products." Tell me how that's going to work to help you create talkable experiences where customers leave with a smile and come back with a friend in tow willing to pay premium pricing?

Mistake #3. Silo Marketing
No Integration Between Marketing and Sales

You've heard me say this before—marketing is not a department, it is a way of being.

Well, that hasn't changed.

What does that mean specifically? It means that the purpose of a marketing department is to constantly upgrade the quality of customers. That means targeting "A" prospects and taking your current "B" customers and making them "A" customers by getting all their business, advising them well so they become lower risk, and getting premium pricing.

That also means that if your marketing department doesn't have an entire plan based on your 3 to 5 segmented, tightly-niched key markets—you are unfocused.

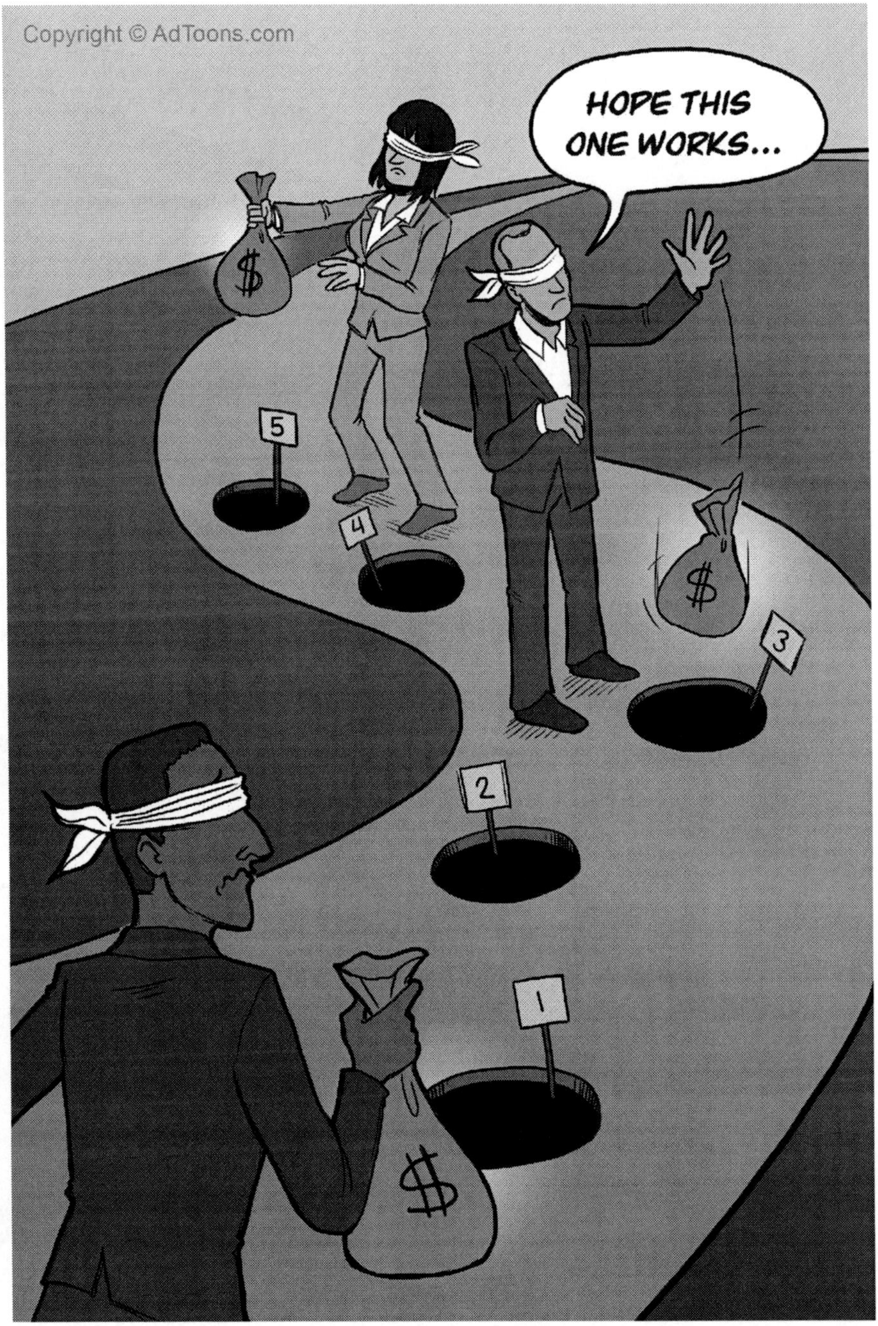
Copyright © AdToons.com
HOPE THIS ONE WORKS...
5
4
3
2
1

If you haven't identified the key prospects in each of those segments, and don't have a targeted one-to-one personalized outreach process to build reputational equity with each one, you are missing the point.

And if you don't have an iron-clad system to track the hand raises from that list and properly direct them through the sales people proven to have the highest closing ratio with the highest premium pricing...well, let's just say whatever *they* ARE doing is a waste.

Your bank doesn't need more unprofitable customers. It's not a numbers game. It's a profit game.

Mistake #4. Abdicating Culture As the Primary Responsibility

Since research shows that the best return on your marketing dollars comes from investment in your people first, followed by investment in customers and then investment to get new prospects, doesn't it make sense that the marketing department needs to be in charge of the culture?

If you're running a "not for profit" bank, then perhaps not. Otherwise, yup, this should be obvious.

Mistake #5. Not Understanding and Managing Strategies Around Net Interest Margin

When I spoke to a group of bank marketers recently, I asked them how many of them understood net interest margin. Not one hand went up.

Whoa, Trigger! Net interest margin is the "it." It's what gets you back out of trouble quickly if you have some problem loans. It's what builds your capital for growth or acquisition. It's your Steady Eddie—the backbone of a healthy bank.

Fees do not automatically renew. RISKY. And legislatures can make fees go away. And every time Congress is in session, you're at risk of having another source of fee income taken away.

RISKIER.

Net interest margin is the gift that keeps giving.

If you and your marketing team don't have solid strategies to get and keep your net interest margin over 5, what rabbit will you pull out of your hat the next time the economy turns worse and you have loan write offs? How will you be ready for the impact of Basel III or what comes next? What will you do to create predictable success that is more important than improving loan quality and net interest margin?

If your marketing team doesn't understand net interest margin, that's not their fault. That is the fault of the executive team for not properly directing the marketing team about the outcomes of their work.

The great news is that all hope is not lost. You and your marketing team can find out that marketing is not a department, but rather, a way of being that everyone in your bank must have.

So drop the "nasty 5," and let's get about having a year filled with a culture of on-fire, clear strategies to get and keep "A+" quality clients, and a net interest margin where all the other banks ask, "How'd they DO that?!"

CHAPTER 8

The Secret Marketing Approach That High-Performing Banks Don't Want You to Know

Shh...there are banks across the country quietly raking in net interest margins of 4, 5 even 6. And THEY don't want YOU to read this.

Before we dive into marketing, let's get clear about what we want marketing to accomplish. To understand that, we have to look at what brings in profit in banking.

This is easy. You already know this one.

What works is bringing in low-risk loans at premium pricing and getting all of their business, while balancing it with substantial core deposit accounts. Period.

That was easy, wasn't it?

Now that we know what makes money in banking, we know what marketing should be doing and how we can measure success.

Okay, okay. That was obvious. Bring in more clients like the 13 percent of current clients who make money for you, and don't market to the rest.

Now what are the highest ROI activities to do that?

Studies Show THIS is the Highest ROI Marketing Activity

First, start with the lowest-hanging fruit. Research shows that having a culture that rocks is the highest ROI marketing activity. In fact, hundreds of studies have confirmed that culture is THE leading predictor of future growth and profitability, so it only makes sense to focus your efforts there.

So, if you spend a boatload on advertising and bring customers in the door, but they don't buy 7 or 8 things on the first visit and rave to others about you—well, that hardly made any sense, now did it?

Your common sense has been screaming this for years. You just thought there was some mystery to marketing, and you didn't get a marketing education while you were busy learning finance.

Copyright © AdToons.com
LIVING THE DREAM!
THE BANK HELPED US BECOME FINANCIALLY INDEPENDENT!
1
BANK
WAY TO GO, DAD!
GOOD JOB, MOM!

So drop the traditional advertising. Instead, invest in your people and make sure you have "talkable" experiences and consistent service.

How to Get Your Customers to Sell for You

And where does the research say you should spend your next dollars? Easy: Spend it with your current customers. Inspiring your customers to bring all their business and all their friends is the next highest ROI activity. That will require an integrated non-marketing marketing approach and a non-sales sales approach. If it feels like marketing or sales, you're doing it wrong. It's about giving above and beyond quantifiable value—far beyond knowing their name and answering phone calls quickly.

Remember, "customer satisfaction" is for lightweights.

Your job is customer *success*.

When you master that, you will have more high-profit business coming at you from every angle.

Now that we have our customer referral and full investment machine going, what's next? It's time to start talking about prospects.

But hold your horses...we don't want ALL prospects. **We want prospects that make money for the bank.** If 87 percent of customers are unprofitable for you, it's elementary that you shouldn't spend money to lose money.

So you'll want to identify the psychographics, firmographics and demographics of profitable customers and define your niches. Now we're talking. Now, and only now, can we start marketing to prospects.

And the great news is that none of the marketing will look like marketing. Gone are the billboards, the radio advertisements, and the "brand" advertisements or "rate" advertisement in the local papers.

Resisting that idea? Let's pull out some uncommon sense and apply it.

If you attract a customer based on a "rate," you have trained them to rate shop and pinch out every penny of profit in every transaction in your relationship.

You can't make that one up on volume.

As for brand advertisement, do me a favor: Count up the number of substantial, high-profit accounts that you pulled in based on your "brand" advertising. Sorry to inflict pain, but sometimes that's what it takes to stop the ingrained beliefs and actions that keep you slavishly following unquestioned patterns that add up to nothing for decades on end.

Just to be clear, let's review. What are the lowest ROI activities? Advertising rates, brand advertising, marketing studies. STOP THEM. They are great ways for marketing firms to profit—but not you.

EmmerichFinancial.com

CHAPTER 9

7 Deadly Sales Mistakes That Crush Your Margin

Before we dive into what you *should* be doing in sales, let's look at the biggest mistakes made by 80% of bank executives who listen to the hue and cry of lenders who just aren't delivering results.

The aggressive and enlightened top-20% executives understand that they've never had more capacity for loan growth at premium pricing in their entire lives.

Why? Because not only is the possibility out there for tremendous loan growth, they also haven't bought into the no-loan-demand story.

Here are seven mistakes that will really constipate your loan growth—now and in the future—and keep you from securing "A+" quality loans at premium pricing. For many banks across America, "A+" loans are the norm, not the exception. If you want to join them, avoid these blunders:

Mistake #1: Expecting People With No Sales Capacity to be Able to Sell.

You can't coach to improve height. People are the height they are. Likewise, some people are naturally inclined from an emotional-intelligence standpoint to want to call on prospects and bring in their business. It's in their blood. It gets them juiced, it gets them jazzed, and they're good at it. This characteristic is innate.

Of course this doesn't mean that skillsets don't matter and that learning to refine sales skills can't drastically help someone who is already naturally inclined to sell. But it does mean that it's really difficult to take a 4-foot-11- inch guy and improve his sales skills by screaming at him, "Why aren't you 7 feet tall!" A different result just ain't gonna happen.

That's why the selection process of hiring into your sales team matters tremendously. And very few banks have done any of their homework in understanding that there exist emotional-intelligence tools which can help them hire the right people.

> **Test-Drive the ONLY emotional-intelligence assessment designed for banks**
>
> *For qualified banks:* Get two free assessments and the 43 key financial industry position benchmarks based on a predictability study, proven to dramatically decrease turnover and increase performance in every position in your bank.
>
> NetInterestMarginSolution.com/ZR

Mistake #2: Calling Everyone.

Dissipating energy is a huge problem for most banks.

Their lenders feel that as long as they are working, that's all that really matters. But working smart is actually what really matters. The key is to convince your lenders that, instead of calling 3,000 business owners, there are really only 30 or so at a time that they should call and bring in as customers. And they should bring in ALL their business, not just part of it. This distinction is a very different mindset, and it's backed by a very different set of behaviors, different discipline, and almost certainly, a different system than the one you have now. Just getting people into the right activity will help you enjoy a breakthrough in loan growth.

Mistake #3: Cold-Calling.

Yes, we've all heard that every good salesperson should be a cold-caller. But think about it: Do you really want your bankers to look like just another schlocky vendor—showing their wares and leaving their brochures? Is that really going to land you premium pricing plus all of that prospect's business? YOU wouldn't buy that way, would you? So why should your prospects?

Instead, select the right prospects and warm them up though warming campaigns that give, give, give so much value that the prospect's incumbent bank starts to look sick. You want these campaigns to solidify in the prospect's mind that you've far exceeded the value their incumbent bank has delivered. Only at that point can your lenders pursue the sales process.

Mistake #4: Sending People Out With a Commodity Mindset.

One of the biggest challenges in banking right now is that salespeople are calling on folks, yet failing to bring in the business--because everything they're offering can be found someplace else. They're "selling" commodity-type products and services.

It's no surprise at this point that the only way salespeople can get business is by matching somebody else's

Copyright © AdToons.com
7 SALES MISTAKES MOST BANKS MAKE
BANK
WHAT DID I DO WRONG?

rate—an even worse scenario than not getting the business at all.

What can you do instead? Create a plethora of unique selling propositions providing superior customer benefits (as I showed you in Chapter 6 of this book). Then, build a sales process around each one—such that every customer or prospect can calculate the money saved or earned from each benefit.

It should be so apparent that these benefits, savings and earnings far exceed—by multiples—the premium pricing that you'll charge them, that "selling" at that point becomes a no-brainer.

Mistake #5: Buying Into Excuses.

The scariest thing I hear is a CEO giving excuses for why their people aren't performing. I can't help thinking, "That's exactly WHY your people aren't performing." Only when I respond, "Thank you for sharing"—then press the CEO to tell me how they can get things done—does their bank begin to change.

When you realize a lot of the banking population is claiming that loan demand has dried up, you can begin to take advantage of the fact that other bankers are sitting around waiting for some body to walk in the door. While they're making excuses, thinking loan demand is not going to recover for a while—you can be out there hustling and bringing in all of their best customers while they are sleeping through that whole thing. Loan growth is all about mindset—and helping your people understand that you won't buy into excuses. The opposite side of excuses is results.

Mistake #6: Measuring Results Only.

You've heard it. You look at the total volume of loans closed and that's the one result that is being discussed, when in fact that is a historic data point. You need data points that are actually input data points to make sure that your next history looks far better.

By not measuring the inputs, most banks end up having really bad outputs. That's why everybody needs to understand the critical drivers, the number of aces achieved with your Top 100 prospects, the number of aces with your Top 1000 prospects, the dollars in the weighted funnel and the cross-sales to current clients that are in the Top 100 best prospects. Those are the kind of measurements that move needles like net interest margin and closed business with A+ credits--and move them quickly. Notice how the traditional "number of sales calls" didn't make the list? Because it's the 1980's solution that didn't work then—and is a abysmal current predictor compared to the others.

EmmerichFinancial.com

Mistake #7: Hoping.

Hope is not a strategy. Measuring, coaching and celebrating, as a pattern and a way of being, is the only way to get to a positive end result.

While most banks think sales training is their answer, nothing could be further from the truth. In fact, in 25 years of working with high-performing banks (and even transforming banks from near closure to the #1 or #2 performer in their state), I've seen repeatedly that those executive teams who do achieve substantial differences understand that their job is to measure, coach, and celebrate...measure, coach, and celebrate...measure, coach, and celebrate. They understand that management is an activity and a process that ties together culture, strategy, marketing, critical drivers, coaching, leadership development and management development. And whenever bankers fail to focus on those activities—thinking that sales training alone will do the trick—they find out in short order that results from sales training have never happened and sales training has never worked...not even once.

Hope is not a strategy. Having an actual strategy is. And a system to support the strategy is the only way to create a huge, profound, and sustainable turnaround.

CHAPTER 10

The 1-Step System Used by Top Banks To Snap *"Rate Shoppers"* Out of Their Preoccupation With Low Rates

If you have kids, you may have had the experience of being on a car trip, driving past waterfalls and canyons and thundering herds of elk, while enduring a constant soundtrack from the back seat: "Are we there yet? Are we there yet?"

They've fixated on the wrong thing: the fact that you'll be swimming in the hotel pool after dinner. Why did you even mention that? You try to explain that what's out the window is the whole point of the trip, the reason you came a thousand miles from home, NOT the hotel pool. You could have traveled five MINUTES back home to swim in a pool.

But you know that until you break their preoccupation with that darn pool, they'll never get the actual benefit of the trip.

The retail sales process is very much the same. A customer calls and asks for your rates. They THINK that what they want is the lowest rate. They are focused like a laser on getting the lowest rate, and they're determined to shop around until they find it. If you give it to them, it would be just like driving straight to the hotel pool at noon. It misses the whole point of giving the customer the highest possible value.

Whenever I hear a salesperson answer a phone and immediately quote rates, I always picture myself lunging across the room in slow motion, saying "NOOOOO!!!"

"But that's what the customer asked for!" he says. Of course it is—that's what customers do, just like a kid in the back seat asking for the hotel pool. But there's more than one way to answer the question, and one of the most important breakthroughs in creating an effective sales culture is breaking the customer's preoccupation with your pricing.

Of course this does no good unless you go on to the second and third and fourth steps because you still need to create your premium pricing and follow the steps to make sure you get all the business. But most people get

Copyright © AdToons.com
RATES, RATES, IT'S ALL ABOUT THE RATES!
WAKE UP! THERE'S MORE!
SLAP

this first step wrong, so let's take a minute to nail that one to the wall.

If you start the sales conversation by quoting rates, you are sending the message that rate is what matters. Worst of all, it's a race to the bottom as you try to match the rate of your most desperate, least worthy competitor—a race you can't win.

Remember just a few short years ago when people got crazy good interest rates on their mortgages from fly-by-night mortgage brokers. Those people no longer own their homes, so it was clear that rate wasn't all that mattered. So did terms...and the small print.

Not only do you hurt the buyer when you don't teach them to make a decision based on value... you lose the ability to develop a deep and sustainable relationship that is instructive on how to make many good financial decisions.

So how do you break the preoccupation with rate? With a break-preoccupation-with-rate question. The formula is that it includes the word "rate" before the word "value," and is followed by a "reason to believe" that value is more important than rate.

Here are a few examples:

"Are you looking for the best rate or the best value? There are about 420 different configurations of mortgages, and most people get the wrong mortgage, which ends up costing more over the course of the loan. Do you mind if I ask you a few questions to make sure we find the mortgage that is the best value for you?"

Or...

"*Are you looking for the best rate or the best value?* There are many different types of CDs these days including those you can add to, take out of, bump rates on, and more. *Do you have time right now so I could ask you a few questions to make SURE we get you the best customized CD and properly structure it to fit the objectives?*"

Now tell me. Would any person of a reasonable IQ answer the questions with, "*I'm not really interested in value—just give me the rate*"? Of course not.

That doesn't mean rate instantly becomes a non-issue for them. If you head off too quickly in a direction they weren't expecting, they might feel suspicious and shut down. So before you start the break preoccupation with rate question, you might want to begin with a reassurance: "Our rates are reasonable and fairly competitive...but tell me.... are you looking for the best rate or the best value? Because..."

That helps them understand you're not deflecting...you're just needing further information to be helpful to them.

What you are doing, of course, is justifying your premium pricing by letting them know how they will benefit from it. You are giving them what they want, even if it isn't instantly apparent to them. You wouldn't expect to pay the same for a new high-performance luxury car that you pay for a 10-year old used family sedan. That's why nobody calls a dealership and says, "What's your price for a car?" Everyone understands that there

EmmerichFinancial.com

are cars, and then there are cars. The same is true of the products and services in your bank. Some things are worth more. Your proper direction and guidance will bring far more value than just schlugging a product at them.

Rate quoting without diagnosis of their situation is malpractice.

Begin the diagnosis by breaking their preoccupation with rate, first and foremost, with a question that always follows the same formula: rate before value, followed by a "reason to believe."

Breaking this preoccupation is by no means the whole sales process. It's a crucial beginning, but it is just the beginning. Without good execution on this first step, you will almost certainly be brought back to the rate conversation and that's a conversation you can't win. Be sure to learn the rest of the No-More-Order-Taking Sales process, then step up to be the professional who deserves their attention as their trusted financial advisor. Do this, and you'll earn their respect and never have them ask for your rate again.

Discover the Complete Formula for Breaking The Preoccupation With Rate

If your people are quoting rates when they should be guiding prospects to premium priced solutions, then round up 5 of your key people and get to the very next Profit-Growth Banking™ Summit.

They'll get fully immersed in the skills and mindset they need to overcome the "rate question," give customers the guidance they deserve and sell at premium pricing.

Details at:
NetInterestMarginSolution.com/Summit.

EmmerichFinancial.com

CASE STUDY

How One Bank Grew Net Interest Margin by 100 Basis Points in Little Over a Year

In banking—as in most other businesses—time is money. So when Legence Bank of Southern Illinois realized they weren't aggressively making needed changes, they had only to look to their ROA for proof that waiting to act had been an expensive decision.

Hiring practices were sketchy, culture was an issue, and some employees had become a costly and unproductive drag on growth. Not only that, but the bank lacked a definitive sales mindset that could demand premium pricing from the marketplace. What's more, they wanted to acquire branches in order to grow. It was easy to see that bringing about change and establishing uniformity in how the branches were run had become not just necessary, but critical—particularly since the recession was in full swing, mega banks were driving customers away, and local competitors were creating opportunities to land top-flight customers as they pulled back on marketing and sales efforts.

In the midst of the turmoil, Legence's President and CEO Kevin Beckemeyer learned about The Emmerich Group's cultural transformation formula through a 190-bank CEO Network he belonged to. Accustomed to seeking out different ways of getting results, Beckemeyer investigated further. Within weeks, he and his executive team made the decision to bring Roxanne Emmerich to Illinois to conduct a Kick-Butt Kick-Off® event to rally their troops and teach a new mindset.

Legence Bank's Top Accomplishments

✓ Net Interest Margin at 5.42 as of June 2014, from 4.94.

✓ Increased ROA from 0.88 to 2.11.

✓ Improved efficiency ration from 75.62% to 58.56%.

✓ Took net income from $1.314 Million to $3.055 Million per year.

✓ Reduced time deposits and grew demand deposits from 8.42 percent to 12.60 percent by targeting large businesses for cash management.

- ✓ Acquired neighboring branch with transition of 60 days or less.
- ✓ Won its county's "Large Business of the Year" distinction.
- ✓ Uses new-hire testing to identify top quality people.
- ✓ Identifies 3 to 5 objectives per year to focus on using Strategic Planning.

> Discover how Legence Bank accomplished such rapid and sustained growth, direct from CEO Kevin Beckemeyer and his executive team…PLUS, watch as Kevin reveals the single biggest impact he and his team have experienced in an exclusive video at NetInterestMarginSolution.com/Resources.

Transformational Mindsets and Systems Were the Key to Acquisition Success and Growth

Soon afterward, the bank formed their own Hoopla Team®[1]—part of Emmerich's formula—to further the work of the Kick-Butt Kick-Off® transformation.

CFO Lynn Bird who runs the Hoopla team, says, *"It's really made a difference. We can now see our team actually*

---

[1] Hoopla Team: The team responsible for rolling out culture changes through quarterly celebrations.

EmmerichFinancial.com

striving to do better in every area—and lifting the bank's numbers in the process. It's something we didn't expect—this enthusiasm on the part of our people—but it's made a huge difference. They're now the real driving force that determines how successful we are...not the economy, the market, not any outside factor. With them playing at this level, I know we can do anything!"

One missing element the Kick-Off identified for Legence was the need for transformational education about how to be—not just what to do—from simple things like how to greet customers, how to answer the phone and how to properly write letters...to more difficult topics like sales and warming campaigns. Once the "how to be" Kick-Off started in earnest, the bank began to see real results. And customers started to rave.

	12/2008	06/2014
Efficiency Ratio	75.62%	58.56%
Return on Assets	.88%	2.11%
Return on Equity	8.67%	17.82%
Net Interest Margin	4.94%	5.42%
Total Assets	149,403	290,157
Net Income	$1.314 Mil	$3.055 Mil *

Legence Bank's growth skyrockets and stays up (*data through June 2014)

Says Beckemeyer, "In every community we're in, we now get so much positive feedback about the enthusiasm and the attention we give our customers. The accolades continue throughout the bank—it's almost contagious. The uniform systems and education from branch to branch is really what has made the good feedback possible."

> "One thing we've learned is not to delay. If we wait around and don't make needed changes, it costs a tremendous amount of money."
>
> —Kevin Beckemeyer, CEO
> Legence Bank

And while some bankers might be cautious about acquiring branches during a "cultural revolution" like this, Legence's early results actually spurred them to start acquiring. By the time acquisition of its first branch was finalized, Legence's Hoopla Team® was so experienced in producing change through training, they were able to convert the existing staff to the new mindset within just 60 days. One customer—a local doctor who had done business with the acquired branch for 30 years and who was familiar with its poor internal culture—congratulated Beckemeyer for the positive change, saying, "I'm not blowing smoke here. You transformed that branch and those people into positive attitudes, smiling faces and helpful employees."

Now that's something every bank CEO likes to hear.

Of course, just like Legence's existing branches, the new branch was expected to meet bankwide growth objectives and benchmarks. Being the "new kid" didn't

EmmerichFinancial.com

count. So when Legence initiated a goal of reducing expensive time deposits in favor of growing demand deposits, all branches pitched in to boost demand deposits from 7 percent to 13 percent.

Targeting large local businesses for cash management was key to the increase.

Now Legence has a cadre of younger lenders hitting the streets calling on potential clients. And the message they're able to deliver to these businesses is one of value-added services—instead of competitive rates. Legence has been able to appeal to prospects by emphasizing innovative services and "total package" lending.

Net Interest Margin Over 5%...Even Competing Against Farm Credit

"We have a lot of farming customers," says Beckemeyer. "We may originate when we compete with Farm Credit. We may have a farm borrower with a large operating loan, large checking accounts—we want the whole relationship in order to remove their other bank from the picture. So we'll combine services including originating a farm real estate loan then selling it in the secondary market...providing a great rate and getting a servicing spread...getting non-interest income from loans, which helps our yield."

110
100
90
80
70
60
50
40
30
20
BASIS POINTS
BANKS
BANKS
Copyright © AdToons.com

Instead of trying to make all its profit on the loan side, Legence works both ends of the spectrum—making money on both loans and deposits.

The bank took seriously the Profit-Rich Sales™ process with many people taking the course repeatedly and using the carefully-crafted unique selling propositions The Emmerich Group helped them create. It wasn't about creating one, but many, all of which spoke to bottom-line impact for the customer.

> *"By using the Unique Selling Propositions in our step-by-step Profit-Rich Sales process that we hold our team to, pricing just isn't an issue anymore. Our clients and employees know we're worth more."*

To stay on track, the bank focuses on three to five objectives every year that they know will make the biggest impact. They even replicate Emmerich's Strategic Planning Think Tank™ process to determine which objectives will help the bank grow in a positive manner.

One objective, for instance, was to improve hiring practices and ensure that the right people are hired for the right roles. Emmerich helped the bank use the ZERORISK Hiring System (free trial for qualified banks at NetInterestMarginSolution.com/ZR) to identify top quality people. According to Beckemeyer, "The only thing that's going to keep us from growing is not hiring the right people."

There are certain people—good people, who are fundamentally incapable of asking to receive 5 percent of the extra hundreds of thousands they bring. They can't be in the position to do that because they will always be the same ones who think nothing of negotiating with you about bringing down the rate.

The culture shift has substantially impacted more than just ROA and other benchmarks—it's changed individuals from the inside out.

People Are Taking Leadership Roles and Making Things Happen

"Some of our team members are different people today— not just in their work lives, but in their personal lives, too. Many of them were kind, dependable and giving—but now they're kind, dependable and giving on steroids. They feel better about their work. Plus, people are taking on leadership roles, breaking out of their shells and making things happen. Our bank is full of people like that," says Beckemeyer. Employees can feel the energy, too, he says. *"I'd love to be fresh out of college, jumping into an atmosphere like this. Our people actually thank us for sending them to the Kick-Butt Kick-Off®.*

We couldn't be more proud of them."

What's his advice for any banker thinking about getting on the High-Performance Happy Bus with Emmerich's program? *"Everybody has to be on board—from the directors all the way to the janitor. If they're not, they magical-*

EmmerichFinancial.com

ly tend to drift away on their own after you have a conversation with them about the new reality."

Those that were on the fence at Legence, he continues, are either fully engaged now or have disappeared on their own.

"Everybody goes to the Profit-Growth Banking™ *Summit and comes back saying, 'This changed my personal life too."* We get that great bankers are great people first and we have many great ones who have become better as a result of this process. With this culture, our CFO, who runs our Hoopla Team® and shapes the culture through it, feels that the sky is the limit. She thinks everything is possible, and based on results she and her team have accomplished so far, she seems to be right!"

Who wouldn't want to stay, enjoy the fun, and get immersed in the new-found, profitable atmosphere?

Finally, a Proven System to Add 40, 60 Even 100 Basis Points to Your Net Interest Margin

You're standing at the abyss. The industry is facing significant, disruptive, changes. Possibly most worrisome among them—the recent revelation in *Fast Company* that Millennials don't think they need a bank.

As if your situation wasn't difficult enough with regulators breathing down your neck, boards of directors screaming for growth and profits and customers nibbling away at your margin one rate-match at a time.

It used to be that banks were stable, *survivor* **businesses—a safe place in the storm.**

Well here's news...the storm clouds are clearing (a little) for everyone else, but not for you. Even though loan demand has inched back up, the pressure to beef up your strategic core deposits and get healthier profits is greater than ever.

If you don't get a grip on it soon, you may be asked to hand the keys to a competitor who's figured it out (we've seen it happen).

There is good news, despite all of your challenges. There are banks getting premium prices every day, in markets big and small, all across the country. We're privileged to work with most of them.

Each is prospering (often at the sad expense of their competitors) by applying what we call *The Franchise System of Banking*.

The Solution that over 114 Bank CEOs have referred to as "A Miracle!"

Profit-Growth Banking™ Summit is the only program that teaches an integrated Strategy, Marketing, Sales, and Service Accountability System "boot camp."

Everything taught here has been proven to work in top and bottom performing banks...

One bank, up on the blocks for sale, became one of the top two performing banks in that state within two years.

Another went from bottom quartile to 18 percent ROE *and* 18 percent organic growth within the first year! Just a few years later, they doubled in size while improving loan quality. Competitors think that can't be done...while they're busy doing it. The competitors just don't know how—they only grow by sacrificing loan quality.

Your biggest risk is *not* attending

We guarantee this will be the most impactful seminar you attend all year or your money back. But I have to caution you...every Summit we've ever held sold out in advance. If you're serious about getting out of the net interest margin vise, go now to:

NetInterestMarginSolution.com/Summit

FREE Resources: Get Tools and Resources to Begin Your Net Interest Margin Transformation

✓ Exclusive video reveals the "magic script" to break a prospect's preoccupation with rate so that you can put the focus on value, not lowest-rate. This is the gateway to premium pricing.

✓ Complete video case-study showing how one bank added 48 basis points to net interest margin…hear directly from the CEO and key executives to discover what they did and how they did it.

✓ Specific, "how-to" articles you can share with your key leaders in retail, marketing and commercial to jump-start your growth.

✓ FREE trial access to the Performance-Accountability course at TGIMU—our multi-million dollar education platform designed specifically for banks—discover the 7 keys to building a culture of performance and accountability.

✓ PLUS: Priority notification of upcoming educational webinars to help you safely and rapidly grow profits and much more…

NetInterestMarginSolution.com/Resources